RECOGNITION RETENTION MADE SIMPLE

2nd Edition

By Dee Armstrong Crabtree

ABOUT THE AUTHOR

Dee Armstrong Crabtree has had by-lines in several periodicals. An accomplished public speaker, she also taught in the Community Learning program at Indiana University and Purdue University at Indianapolis (IUPUI). Ms. Crabtree previously served as the record retention manager for a *Fortune 500* company.

OTHER BOOKS BY THIS AUTHOR

A Simply Wonder Life: A Guide to Easy Organization

A Simply Wonderful Holiday

Record retention Made Simple, First Edition

Promise Road

Uncle Imblay's Fortune

Simply Wonderful Sailing

COPYRIGHT INFORMATION

Copyright 2019, Dee Armstrong Crabtree

All rights

ISBN: 9781792898037

Imprint: Independently published

AUTHOR NOTE

This manual is designed to guide you through the intimidating challenges of creating and managing a comprehensive record and information management (RIM) program. Here you will find all of the resources you need to get your program up and running.

What you won't find in these pages are a lot of industry facts and figures that will are irrelevant to the design of your program. Likewise, I will not bore you with a detailed examination of the science or the history of recordkeeping. You will not find legal advice within these pages. For legal advice regarding RIM program design, please contact an attorney who specializes in your particular industry.

What you will find in this book are detailed instructions on how to design and build the complete program, from creating the basic building blocks that will constitute a solid foundation, up to and including how to manage the entire life of the program. The corresponding worksheets found in the appendices will help you organize and document each step of your program's design.

TABLE OF CONTENTS

1) Why do You Need a Program?
2) The Chicken or the Egg: Which Step Comes First?
3) You're the RIM Manager: Now What?
4) Support from the Top
5) Gathering the Generals
6) Rallying the Troops
7) The Policy at the Heart of it All
8) The Hardest Part: The Records Inventory
9) The Scariest Part: The Schedule
10) Your Storage Vendor: Your Partner
11) Legal Hold Systems
12) Out with the Old: Destruction Processes
13) Training the Staff
14) The Big Rollout
15) Inspiring and Ensuring Compliance
16) The Future: Day-to-Day Program Management

APPENDICES

- A. The Master Plan
- B. The Executive Team
- C. Department Heads and Records Administrators
- D. Record Inventory Form
- E. Sample Schedule
- F. Off-Site Vendor Questionnaire
- G. Training Records
- H. Compliance Certification Form
- I. Audit Tracking

CHAPTER ONE
WHY DO YOU NEED A PROGRAM?

In this era of stringent legislation and excessive litigation, every business needs an effective and consistently enforced record management system that encompasses both paper and digital records. The problem is that few business owners or managers know how to create a system that will enable them to efficiently manage their records and that will at the same time provide the solid legal protection that might be needed in the face of litigation or an audit.

The consequences of not having a solid RIM plan are formidable, but unfortunate truth is that the great majority of American enterprises completely lack any sort of RIM program. Failure to create and/or adhere to a record retention policy can, and sometimes does, lead to severe damage to the reputation of a business, a jeopardized financial future and even potential prison sentences for executives who fail to comply with government regulations. On a more positive note, the implementation and consistent enforcement of a well-designed program can save any business a great deal of time and money.

Awareness of the need for a RIM Program is most often born when a corporate board member or a business manager reads a newspaper article about the perils of failing to have a such program in place. The task of designing the program most often falls upon the shoulders of legal or operational staff who may have no knowledge whatsoever about creating or enforcing the policy and procedures.

We are a nation drowning in records, both paper and electronic. Predictably, decades-old corporations can accrue huge volumes of paper over time, often needlessly paying for the storage of long forgotten records. The costs of record creation and storage, regardless of the format, are soaring. The paperless society that we were all promised still eludes us in many ways. While digital storage of records is much more cost effective than hard copy storage, some regulations dictate that certain paper records be stored over an extended period of time.

Confusion abounds over the many complex regulatory issues that govern how long each record must be kept. Many enterprises must adhere to guidelines established by the Department of Labor, the Internal Revenue Service, the Sarbanes–Oxley Act and the Fair Debt Collection Practices Act, just to name a few. Determining which regulations must be adhered to can be an intimidating assignment for any RIM manager.

However, the most daunting aspect of RIM program design is often just knowing where to start. First and foremost, what constitutes a record? Who regulates your records and what do those regulations stipulate? What records are needed to ensure business continuity during times of crisis? What essential information must be covered in the company RIM policy? How should the retention schedule be structured? How and where should records be archived? How will records be protected and retrieved in the face of litigation? Where do you begin to manage the mountain of records that even the tiniest business can generate?

Every RIM program revolves around the same basic components regardless of the industry in which the business is involved and regardless of the format. Every RIM program must:

- Start with a well-defined retention policy;
- Feature an all-inclusive record retention schedule the includes both paper and digital records;
- Be well-publicized to all employees;
- Provide in-depth training for all employees;
- Provide a system for monitoring records inventory;
- Mandate company-wide compliance;
- Feature a concise litigation hold system; and
- Provide for systematic final disposition of all records.

The risks faced by any business failing to institute and maintain an effective RIM program are immense. While RIM programs are not new, regulation and enforcement issues have changed over the past few years and they continue to evolve at a breakneck pace. In particular, changes in the rules of discovery have pushed RIM programs into the realm of the essential for every business.

While most courts do not dictate how a RIM program must be structured, they do examine *good faith intentions* in the areas of implementation and enforcement. Judges most often question whether the company has consistently followed its own dictates. Were retention and destruction processes carried out according to the posted schedule? Were legal holds issued and honored? Was the review and audit program faithfully executed? Were regulatory guidelines followed?

In addition to risk mitigation, there are cost considerations. On-site storage can consume valuable real estate. Off-site storage can consume a considerable amount of the budget. Failure to centralize and manage records inventory with well-defined compliance guidelines can result in multiple boxes of irrelevant records being stored for decades. Mid-to-large size companies can spend thousand and thousands of dollars annually for both on-site and off-site storage of countless documents. Employees come and go, some of whom unfortunately take their knowledge of the stored records with them, leaving the records behind, often lost and forgotten, yet still costing the company money.

Scare tactics aside, there are numerous benefits to having a strong, effective RIM program. Diligent managers can expect decreased storage and discovery costs, increased ability to preserve and locate records, mitigated risk in the face of litigation and audits, assured compliance with federal and state laws, improved disaster recovery capabilities and notable improvement in the areas of customer service and performance.

Having a centralized, enterprise-wide RIM program is vital, but it need not be difficult to create or manage such a program. A first-rate program will ultimately bring order to the company and peace of mind to the company's management team.

Four, *Support from the Top*, will assist you in getting the backing that you absolutely must have.

Step Two: Establish an Executive Committee

Once you have the blessing of management, it is time to establish a high-level team of managers who know your business inside and out. The most well-rounded team will include a ranking member from each division or department. Identify and recruit your most significant stakeholders as they will have a vested interest in your program and will eventually become your true champions. See Chapter Five, *Gathering the Generals*, for guidelines on how to establish your executive committee.

Step Three: Develop the Core Policy

New you will develop an overall policy regarding the day-to-day handling of the company's records. The basic tenets of the policy should provide the groundwork for your recordkeeping process. Chapter Seven, *The Policy at the Heart of it All*, will walk you through the key points that should be included in the policy.

Step Four: Conduct a Record Inventory

Conducting the record inventory is the most time-consuming part of the process. It is also the step that demands your utmost attention. During this process, you will identify exactly what records the company generates and determine what the lifecycle is for each of those records. Chapter Eight, *The Hardest Part: The*

Records Inventory, will guide you through this monumental task.

Step Five: Create the Retention Schedule

If conducting the record inventory is the most time-consuming step, then developing the retention schedule is the most intimidating. During this phase, you will review the various laws and regulations, as well as contractual obligations, that govern your business. Using that information, you will document the decisions you and your committee make regarding retention periods. See Chapter Nine, *The Scariest Part: The Schedule*, for details.

Step Six: Select a Storage Vendor

Most companies have more records then they can safely store on-site. See Chapter Ten, *Your Storage Vendor: Your Partner*, for guidance on how to select a vendor and reap the most out of the services that the selected vendor can provide.

Step Seven: Develop a Legal Hold System

The development of a legal hold system is a simple but crucial step. You must work with your legal team to create a hold process that is both effective and easy to implement. For guidelines on how to create the hold process, see Chapter Eleven, *Legal Hold Systems*.

Step Eight: Define Document Destruction Procedures

When records expire, it is important to have a plan for their final destruction. Whether or not a company's record destruction process has been carried out in a timely manner is a key factor in litigation and audit matters. See Chapter Twelve, *Out with the old: Destruction Procedures*, for information regarding this important process.

Step Nine: Train the Staff

All of your hard work will be for naught unless you provide in-depth training to your staff. It is vital that all employees fully comprehend the record retention policy and established procedures. For help on developing your training program, see Chapter Thirteen, *Training the Staff*.

Step Ten: The Big Rollout

One you have all of the pieces of your master plan in place, it will be time to host a special day to kick-off your new program. If you want to command attention and inspire enthusiasm, you will need to infuse your pre-release communications with a lot of energy. Learn how to do that in Chapter Fourteen, *The Big Rollout*.

Step Eleven: Build on Your Momentum

To keep your program effective, you must vigilantly monitor and manage ongoing companywide compliance. Each and every employee must regard

RIM as a vital part of their duties. Read about how to inspire compliance in Chapter Fifteen, *Inspiring and Ensuring Compliance*.

Step Twelve: Day-to-Day Management

Your work does not stop after the kickoff. In fact, every day you must oversee security, retrieval processes, preservation, audits, litigation holds and record destruction. In addition, you must continually review the established policy and procedures to ensure that they meet the company's ever-changing needs and you will need to devise plans for improvement as the business evolves. Refer to Chapter Sixteen, *The Future: Day-to-Day Program Management*, for advice on keeping it all together.

CHAPTER THREE
YOU'RE THE RIM MANAGER: NOW WHAT?

The strength of any RIM program relies upon the strengths of the program manager. RIM initiatives succeed only when a qualified, knowledgeable manager takes the helm. The ultimate responsibility of inspiring and ensuring companywide compliance by providing ongoing leadership, education and guidance is yours.

You must be a proactive team leader. A successful RIM program manager will collaborate with executive management to initiate the program, middle management to implement it and administrative staff to manage it on a regular basis.

In principle, your position should be considered a service position. In preeminent programs, the RIM managers work with each and every department in order to help them comply with the dictates without impeding their operational goals. This frequently involves one-on-one consultations regarding document lifecycle management. You should be readily available to answer any questions and address all concerns regarding policies, retention schedules and internal processes. You might be called on to settle occasional disputes. You must be ready to offer easily implemented solutions and alternatives to whatever problems that come your way.

To be truly effective, you must possess a wide range of business acumen, operational awareness and communication prowess. You need to develop a thorough understanding of work flow and business processes throughout the company. For example, when a company contracts for landscaping, who becomes the primary custodian of that contract after it has been signed by both parties and how long must it be kept on file?

Should the contract be sent to the legal department? Does it belong to the procurement staff that negotiated the deal? Should it go to the building services area that oversees the services provided under that contract? Ownership of all company records should be clearly delineated within the policy as it is determined with the guidance of legal counsel and business unit managers.

You should also be ready and able to mediate all disputes regarding cross-departmental recordkeeping responsibilities. It will be up to you to document the rationale behind custodial and retention decisions.

You must have the ability to effectively communicate to all parties the company policy directives, as well as the established management practices and procedures. You must be able to work with all levels of staff, from the mail courier to the CEO, to facilitate full understanding and compliance with the program.

Strong communication and training skills are essential for a RIM manager. Employees simply cannot comply with what they cannot comprehend. It is your duty to verify that everyone who works for the company, regardless of their capacity, understands and complies with the established policies and procedures.

CHAPTER FOUR
SUPPORT FROM THE TOP

While getting the support of the company's top leadership is the first essential step in creating your program, it should be one of the easiest steps. Your CEO was most likely the person who mandated the program, so he has probably been on your side from the very beginning.

However, most CEOs are swamped with multiple demands. If the RIM program wasn't his brainchild, you will have to be proactive in obtaining his support. You want to make it as easy as possible for him to give you his outspoken backing. That support must come in writing and it must be addressed to other top tier management members.

The key is to approach your leader with the final written document in-hand. That might mean hard copy actually in-hand or it could be in the form of an email. The method you use will depend on the culture of the company, as well as your CEO's management style.

What to put into that support memo? Put everything you need to run your program into that vital manuscript. By everything, I don't mean budget, equipment, software or anything tangible. What you most need is the full support and cooperation of all the managers. You must have full compliance from all the employees. You want everyone on-board with the program with absolute enthusiasm. Finally, you need for your authority to run the program to be firmly and clearly stated.

Your support documentation should be a persuasive missive explaining why the program is being instituted, stressing the important of full compliance and emphasizing how every employee will benefit from the initiative. I urge you not to make it more difficult than it needs to be. Keep the style simple and straightforward. Keep it short and resist the temptation to fill with legalese. Long and boring memos simply just are not read by the vast majority of people.

Your support document may well be the first introduction that managers throughout the company will receive regarding the RIM program. The introduction should be convincing but brief, gathering interest for your exciting new undertaking. Stress that total involvement in this program is imperative for countless financial, operational and legal reasons.

Take this opportunity to establish yourself as the RIM manager and as the future contact for any RIM concerns and/or questions. Finally, coach the managers to compel total cooperation from every member of their team.

Once you have refined the support document, take it to your leader for approval and confirm what conduit should be used to convey this message to the top managers. Then do everything in your power to facilitate that communication. If your program is going to be legitimized, it is crucial that this support request to the managers go out under the CEO's signature.

CHAPTER FIVE
GATHERING THE GENERALS

You've undoubtedly heard the cliché, *Strike while the iron is hot*. It may be cliché but that is exactly what you need to do. Take your next step within 24-hours of the publication of the support document. Recruit executive committee members during those first crucial hours, while the message remains fresh in their minds. Do not underestimate their importance in the success of the program. The executive team can assist with the creation and continued revisions of the retention schedule and can offer priceless program publicity and support, as well.

Search out high-level managers who will likely be the major stakeholders. Seek out the widest possible variety of in-house expertise that is available. Your team should be well-rounded. Look first to the legal, accounting, operational and IT departments. Not only will their motivation for participation differ but the expertise they bring to your table will differ, as well.

The legal department can provide guidance as to the laws and regulations that must be observed, such as Sarbanes–Oxley. Recruit your highest-level accounting executive as the records managed by that department are the heart and soul of the company. Information about those records is crucial to your success. Finally, the folks in the operational areas may surprise you with their hands-on knowledge of the records that move the business, regardless of whether you're processing loan applications or fulfilling product orders.

One *caveat* to remember is that your committee should remain small. Too many committee members will muddle the process. Select the best representative from each department, then hone that person's particular talents. Select participants who are known producers. Everyone on your team must be a workhorse. Your RIM program is no fit place for show horses, *i.e.*, people who are all talk and no action. On the same note, while it can be a high-profile opportunity for you, it is important that you concentrate on getting things done, not showcasing yourself. Don't let your ego or your ambition stand in the way of creating the best program for the company's needs.

Your program will be a strange new arena to some of the committee members you select. It is important to clearly define the direction and program goals at the beginning. Once you have assembled the team, you may find that some members will try to take over and direct the program to suit their needs. While you should accommodate those needs whenever possible, you must manage the committee; don't let them manage you. The major stakeholders need to let you know how your program will affect them but do not let them drive the program or impede your progress with their uncertainty and hesitancy.

It will be best if the first meeting is a face-to-face with the entire group. If the company is spread across several locations, try to avoid the cost of travel by utilizing video conferencing. Provide each member with a copy of the presentation prior to the meeting. The copy provided will serve as a handbook of sorts.

So, what should go into the presentation? First, provide a short but detailed outline of the overall goals for the program, as well as a generalized timeline for implementation. The next section will detail the duties of each of committee member. What those duties entail is up to you. However, I would suggest that you include all of the team members in the process of policy creation and the review of the various regulations that govern your business. Pick their brains about the variety of records that are essential to their departments and what their operational concerns are. The executive committee members can inform you of their business needs and litigation risks. They may also have information about the types of programs and services already in use throughout the company, which could prevent you from wasting money on unnecessary duplication of efforts. Allow plenty of time at the end of your initial presentation for questions and answers because there will be lots of questions.

Give each team member a rough sketch of the basic policy you have drafted and ask them to review it before the next meeting. Establish the date, time and place of your next meeting before you send them on their way. In fact, you would do well to schedule a series of recurring meetings on a weekly or monthly basis leading up to implementation day to get input as you progress through each step of the program development.

Use the worksheet in Appendix B to guide you in developing your executive team.

CHAPTER SIX
RALLYING THE TROOPS

The creation of a RIM program is a much bigger task than can or should be managed by one person. Even though you must start at the top, every employee eventually becomes a part of the RIM team. Not only do you need the buy-in of top management, you also need the cooperation of middle management and the entire staff.

To gain that cooperation, you must create a working team of department heads (DHs) and records administrators (RAs). They will serve as important liaisons. The DHs and RAs will consist of the major stakeholders, including managers, and front-liners in the RIM program.

The RIM program is often seen as a troublesome and confusing issue that employees don't have the time or the inclination to deal with. If you are managing the RIM program for a large company, you simply won't have time to meet with each and every employee to provide badly needed guidance. However, having your liaisons in place will resolve that issue. They can provide the handholding that you can't.

One problem that often arises in RIM programs is that the people who work hands-on with the records are not consulted at the start, which can result in unforeseen problems in the long run. The executives may have the best overview of contractual and legal obligations, but the assistants are often the only ones who know the important details of the records each area handles. Stress to the DHs and RAs how important their involvement truly is. During the DH and RA selection process, if at all possible, ask your CEO to proffer the invitation to team members, adding import and authority to their appointment.

Make sure that each team member knows that they were individually selected to be a part of the RIM team because of the skills and abilities that they possess. Impress upon them that being a part of this team is a very important company function. In every communication with these groups, use the title *Record and Information Management Team* or *RIM Team*. In order for each group to respect the other and to understand each other's role in the process, train them as one group. Any time you consult with a DH for any given department, be sure to include the RA in that meeting and *vice versa*. Promote the team concept at every turn, stressing the value of everyone's contribution.

The consultations with your team should start early in the process. When conducting the records inventory, take the opportunity to learn about the needs of various departments and their ideas for the program. Discussing the RIM program with participants during the development stages will reap many benefits for you and the program. Fully understanding the processes and needs of each group will ease concerns and avert problems before they arise.

Do not underestimate how vital RAs are to the record retention team. Not only will they process records for long-term storage but they will also serve as their department's on-site expert, guiding members of their department regarding which records to keep and which records to dispose of.

As a member of the team, they will be asked to learn the program backwards and forwards so that they can answer questions that might otherwise be directed to you. RAs need to know the ins-and-outs of the policy. They need to understand the terms. They need to know the procedures. They should be given authority over their department's records and be able to provide leadership to others in their departments. Finally, they will oversee the destruction of expired records.

DHs also serve an important role. They will interact with you to keep you abreast of changes in contractual obligations, legislation or operations that might necessitate changes to the schedule. They will also be the ones with signing authority when it comes time to destroy records because destruction usually comes out of the budget of department responsible for the records to be destroyed.

Every month, short emails should go out to all DHs and RAs to advise them of upcoming events, new processes and retention schedule changes. See Chapter Thirteen for details on training your team. See Appendix C for a worksheet to help you keep track of who your DHs and RAs are.

CHAPTER SEVEN
THE POLICY AT THE HEART OF IT ALL

Think of your RIM policy as a giant umbrella. In order to protect the company's long-term best interests, you have to cover all of the potential issues under that one umbrella. Your policy should clearly address the most basic questions and concerns of your employees. As ridiculous as it might seem, you will even have to define what constitutes a record within your organization.

Once your executive team has been established, the first team project will be to develop the basic policy. While you should seek the input of your executive committee, drafting the bones of the policy prior to the first team meeting will help point the team in the right direction at the very beginning. If you don't present the team with a basic policy, along with the rationale for it, the group will lack a clear vision what needs to be accomplished.

The first draft of the policy will set the tone and establish the over-all goals for the program. There is no set format for retention policies but several good examples can be found on the Internet. While you should not blindly adapt any of those policies in whole, you can adopt the basics of the better examples that you find. Pay particular attention to those policies issued by the government because they naturally follow the most stringent government regulations.

When writing the policy, review the company's general stated goals and other established policies.

The RIM policy should be tailored to fit within the company's unique culture. Consider what you ultimately want the program to look like. You want to ensure that your RIM program leads to reduced cost and increased efficiency, as it certainly has the potential to achieve both.

In order to ensure that your individualized policy is compliant with current regulations and that you are doing all that you can to mitigate risk, include the following in the policy:

1. An official explanation of what constitutes a record. Talk to your legal advisor as to what that might be in your particular industry.
2. The difference between a business use copy and an official archival version.
3. Instructions to employees to dispose of drafts once a final version of any record is approved. Likewise, discourage the retention of duplicate electronic and paper copies of records. Asking employees to rely mostly on electronic versions as opposed to paper can result in major cost savings for the company.
4. A ban on retaining documents that can be easily obtained elsewhere, *i.e.*, research articles that can be pulled from the Internet at any time.
5. How to determine who is responsible for the long-term retention of any given record.
6. Whether or not employees are allowed to keep personal records on-site. Most retention

policies ban the storage of employees' personal papers on-site as a matter of practicality.
7. Instructions as to whether employees are allowed to keep old planners/calendars or other *just in case* files.
8. Directions on how to properly dispose of expired or unnecessary records, such as multiple copies of the same documents.
9. A reference to where the retention schedule can be located. If the policy is released prior to the completion of the retention schedule, note that in your policy draft and provide the schedule's anticipated publication date.
10. A clear explanation of the legal hold process.
11. If you use off-site storage, include the specifics as to what records should be stored off-site, the cost and the procedures.
12. The contact information for the RIM manager, along with a note encouraging records handlers to reach out with any questions or concerns that they may have.

It is impossible to inspire cooperation when employees are struggling to understand the scope of the project, let alone appreciate the importance of it. In order to facilitate nearly universal understanding, the average news article is written at the seventh-grade reading level. Record retention policies must be written at that same level to guarantee enterprise-wide understanding.

Terms such as retention period and retention schedule should be clearly defined. For example, when does the retention for any given record begin? What if the record type isn't on the retention schedule? Simply put, it is the job of the program manager to make records management as straightforward and simple as possible.

Once the policy has been thoroughly defined at an easily comprehensible level, it should be well-publicized company-wide. The policy should be posted on the company Intranet and all employees should receive an email announcing the posting. If an Intranet page is not available, the policy and schedule should be emailed to each employee. It should also be distributed to all new hires.

Your policy should be as well-known to your employees as your code of business conduct is. They need to be thoroughly educated about their responsibilities and the consequences they face if they fail to carry out those responsibilities.

CHAPTER EIGHT
THE HARDEST PART:
THE RECORDS INVENTORY

Conducting a survey of all the records processed by the company is the most time-consuming aspect of the process, but it can also be the most interesting aspect. During this state, you will meet with department heads and staff from all over the company and learn exactly how their work fits into everyday operations. When you meet with the department heads, include some of their front-line workers in the meeting because those staffers often have the best working knowledge of the lifecycle of the records. You will also be conducting interviews with both the creators and the end-users of the records processed in each department. By the time that you complete this process, you will be uniquely and thoroughly aware of how the company functions.

This is the ideal time to generate RIM program interest and enthusiasm out on the frontline. By interviewing both management and staff, you are demonstrating an interest in how they operate, what their needs are and how the RIM program can save them time and money.

Depending on the size of the company, this phase can last anywhere from days to months. Your first step is to identify department heads, then schedule meetings with them and select members of their staff. During these meetings, you will discuss every paper and electronic record that is created by or that passes through that department. Take several copies of the worksheet found in Appendix D along with you to these meetings.

You will complete one worksheet for every record type that each department creates or processes. This questionnaire will help you document each record's creator, purpose and life cycle. You will also learn who the ultimate conservator for each record is and the necessary format for that record.

For example, let's take a look at expense reports. In this scenario, an employee creates an expense report and then sends it to the supervisor for approval. The supervisor approves it and sends it on to accounting. The accounting department then processes the report and reimburses the employee for the expenses listed on the report. Accounting then stores the expense report and receipts for seven years, the generally accepted accounting standard. Make note of all of the pertinent information, then diagram the process. The inventory sheet you create for the expense report should look something like the example on the following page:

RECORD INVENTORY FORM

Name of document: Employee Expense Report

Created by: Employee Name

Submitted to: Supervisor Name

Processed by: Accounting

Storage location: Accounting Department files

Active retention period: One month

Archive retention period: Seven years

Governing rule, if known: IRS standard

Contractual obligation, if any: None

Process diagram

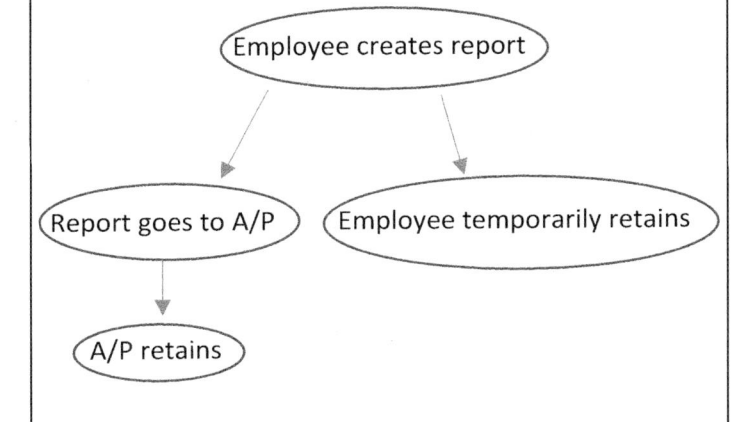

```
          Employee creates report
           /              \
          ↓                ↓
  Report goes to A/P    Employee temporarily retains
          ↓
     A/P retains
```

Once you've conducted your due diligence within the department, document the date of the meeting(s), the names of the staff members present and make note of any pertinent questions or issues that arose during the meeting. Send the summary and copies of the inventory forms to the department heads involved and ask them to sign off on the project and to return the approved forms to you. This step need not be formal. A simple email asking the department head to review and confirm the information contained on the inventory sheets is all that is needed.

Create a file and archive all of the inventory forms submitted. Not only will you use these sheets in the next steps but a day may come when you will have to justify your decisions in court and records could save the day.

CHAPTER NINE
THE SCARIEST PART:
THE SCHEDULE

If conducting the records inventory is the most time-consuming step, then developing the record retention schedule is the most intimidating. During this phase, you will review the various laws, regulations and contractual obligations that govern your business.

Your retention schedule is that vital document that defines what company records should be kept, how long they should be retained and the format in which that are to be stored. The schedule will also detail the primary custodian of each record, along with the rational that was used to establish the proper retention period. As you draft the schedule, document the decisions that are made regarding retention periods, as well as the justification.

This is the phase of RIM program creation that makes managers the most nervous. However, you need not worry as much as you might think. Most courts look not so much as to whether or not proper retention periods have been established but whether the company had good reason for establishing the retention periods as they did and if they have faithfully followed their own guidelines, as defined within the policy.

Now is when you grab those folders that were created during the records inventory phase and start to bring some order to the chaos. The simpler you keep the retention schedule, the more likely it is that the employees will comply with its directives. Again, employees cannot comply with what they cannot comprehend.

The best format for a RIM schedule is a functional one. In a functional format, the record types are broken down into broad categories such as accounting, real estate, contracts, etc. By grouping several related record types together in these broad categories, it is to keep the number of record categories down to a manageable minimum. Aim for utilizing 100 record types or less. Anything much more than that and the schedule will be cumbersome and confusing.

You can buy any number of expensive software programs that will help create a record retention schedule, but a simple spreadsheet should allow all of the flexibility and functionality that is needed. An example of a good basic retention schedule can be found in Appendix E. Using this example, start by establishing the basic groups that the company needs. Almost every company, regardless of the industry, will need divisions for accounting, historical, legal and personnel records. Once you've established the major divisions needed, assign each one a color, such as red for accounting, blue for personnel, etc. Using color at this stage will be a major timesaver on down the road.

Next, review the record inventory forms that you've collected. As you go through each sheet, determine which category each one falls under and either mark it with a colored tag or drop it into a color folder for that category. Once this process is done, go back through and enter them onto the spreadsheet, putting them under the appropriate division. At this point, you will most likely have far more than the prescribed 100 record types, because each type will be a separate line item. At a later date, you will further refine the schedule by grouping like records.

As you create each line item, fill in all of the information you have for each record type. For many lines, you will not yet know the retention period. Those will be established later.

Next comes the research phase. It will be necessary to research the company's retention obligation for each record type. Some retention periods are established by contracts the company has entered into. Some retention periods are governed by law. Some are determined strictly by business need.

Where do you go to find the answers? There are several great resources that can help you find the information you seek. Your legal department, your executive committee and your department managers may already have that information. Government websites often provide solid guidelines. If none of these sources have the answer, you may need to consult an outside attorney for advice on special matters.

One thing you will need to note on the retention schedule is the difference between working copies and archival copies of most records. Working copies are generally kept for as long as there is an active need for them. Archival copy retention periods are clearly defined by the established and posted schedule.

For example, let's revisit the inventory sheet we created for an employee expense report, which reflects the lifecycle of that particular record. As you can see, the employee retains a copy of the original report that he sends to his supervisor. However, since accounting is the established primary custodian of the record (according to the company schedule) the question becomes how long should the employee retain his copy, if he really needs to keep a copy at all.

One of the finest features of a consistently enforced RIM program is that it eliminates costly and inefficient duplication of record storage efforts. The accounting department is the primary custodian. Therefore, it would be a waste of valuable resources for the employee to keep the record any longer than necessary. This is where the term *business purpose need* comes into play. In this case, the employee only needs to keep his copy until he has been reimbursed. In fact, if expense reports are created electronically, employees should be encouraged to rely solely on the electronic copy, thus avoiding the costs of printing and storing paper copies. Should the employee have an unexpected need for the record in the future, accounting, as the primary custodian, would be responsible for supplying the employee with a copy upon request.

Once the first draft of the retention schedule has been created, call a meeting of the executive committee. The purpose of this meeting will be to refine the schedule. Send each member of the committee your draft schedule and the newest draft of the company policy well in advance of the meeting. Ask each member to review both documents prior to the meeting so that they will be ready to make comments and suggestions when you sit down together.

After the committee defines the retention periods, combine like records with like retention into large groups. For example, the accounting category can be a broad one, including invoices, receipts and other related records.

Once the schedule has been refined into a final format that everyone agrees on, send it to the executive committee for the final input and/or approval.

When the finalized schedule has received approval from executive management, publicize and publish it for your employees according to your normal policy distribution procedures, whether that be on the company Intranet or *via* hard copy. Post it along with an admonition that these retention periods must be strictly adhered to. Include details of the ramifications for non-compliance.

The retention schedule will always be a fluid document, subject to change as laws, contractual obligations and business needs change. Best practices dictate that schedule be reviewed on an annual basis to confirm that it still meets the company's needs.

CHAPTER TEN
YOUR OFF-SITE STORAGE VENDOR:
YOUR PARTNER

Many companies use off-site storage vendors for the storage of records that they must maintain but that they don't necessarily need access to every day. What many companies fail to realize is that an off-site storage vendor, in addition to providing storage, can also be a valued partner when it comes to controlling records inventory and cutting costs. Many of these storage vendors off highly valuable services, such as monitoring and destruction services, in addition to record warehousing.

It is best to utilize one centralized vendor in order to prevent the program from becoming fragmented and difficult to monitor. Chaos ensues when one department uses one vendor and another department uses a different one. Several national off-site storage vendors have locations in almost every major metropolitan area. Using a single vendor for all off-site storage services facilitates centralization and allows better control over the entire records inventory, and most service providers will bundle their services in order to provide an economical and effective program.

Before looking into expensive software or cloud-based inventory tracking systems, ask the off-site vendor if they have similar systems available that will do the job. The biggest and best vendors offer free on-line tracking systems that can save you thousands of dollars. These systems allow companies to detail what records are sent off-site, order storage boxes, track record movement and ultimately order destruction. These reporting systems also help ease the audit process by providing reports that can be broken down by department and/or record types.

When selecting an off-site storage vendor, conduct a thorough due diligence process to ensure that you ultimately select the most secure and economical service available. When searching for the right vendor, there are several factors to take into consideration. Appendix F provides a list of questions to ask when considering a new service provider.

First, do a site visit to any potential provider under consideration. Look for security fences surrounding the facility, as well as security cameras. Ask about the vendor's fire protection system. Inquire as to what type of background checks they perform on their employees. Ask to see how records are processed once brought into the facility. Look at the vendor's delivery trucks and ask about the security procedures while records are being delivered. In short, make sure that records are 100% secure from the minute the box is picked up from your facility until it is returned to you or eventually destroyed.

Ask to test drive the vendor's on-line system. Most vendors will encourage you to do just that as a part of their sales presentation. It could be that a vendor who charges more per square for storage might actually be the wiser choice if their on-line management system meets your needs better than that of lower priced competitors.

Appendix F provides a list of questions to ask potential vendors.

CHAPTER ELEVEN
LEGAL HOLD SYSTEMS

The legal hold system is where all of the hard work and due diligence that was invested in creating the new program will be tested and proven. Legal holds are instituted when the company receives a summons, an audit notice or any similar documentation request. Creating a well-organized, easy to implement legal hold system is central to the success of the program. It is where your program will sink or swim. This is where you can actively demonstrate the value of the program to management.

Your best friend during this step of program creation should be your legal advisor, regardless of whether she is on-staff or hired from outside the company. Not only should your legal counsel guide you through the creation of the hold system but she should also oversee the process when the need arises, advising which records should be placed under the hold order and should also designate which employees should receive the notice.

Once the company receives a summons or a notice, the attorney in charge of the litigation or the chief officer overseeing the audit should draft a hold notice. The notice should include:

> ➢ An explanation as to why the notice is being issued, including a brief description of the investigation or suit;

- What records should be held and for how long;
- The ramifications of non-compliance:
- Who is responsible for protecting the affected records;
- A request that the recipient of the notice acknowledge receipt; and
- Contact information for questions and/or where to send requested records.

The text of the notice should be simple and straightforward, stating that all records related to the specific matter, regardless of where they stand in the retention period, should be retained until further notice. Once the notice has been drafted, oversee the distribution of the notice to the appropriate employees. Distribute the notice only to the necessary parties, not to all employees, as you will be tracking all individual acknowledgements of the hold order.

The attorney in charge will determine when to release the hold. Once the hold is released, advise all employees that all records previously being held under the notice may be returned to storage and resume their normal retention period.

Legal hold processes are not difficult but it is crucial to carefully implement and monitor the process when the need arises. The consequence of non-compliance with this part of your RIM program could be devastating to the company, whether those consequences come in the form of court sanctions or the loss of an economically devastating lawsuit.

CHAPTER TWELVE
OUT WITH THE OLD:
DESTRUCTION PROCESSES

In previous chapters, we've discussed how to determine what records to keep and how long to keep them. What should be done with records when they reach the end of their designated retention period? That's exactly what your co-workers will ask you and that is why you need to design and define the destruction processes well before the implementation of the program.

Routine, consistent destruction of expired documents will save the company money and mitigate risk. Clearly delineating destruction process for your employees will ensure that consistency.

Overseeing and documenting the destruction process demands strong attention from you as the program manager. If the company is embroiled in litigation, it is crucial that you be able to prove to the court that your destruction procedures are consistent with your policy and the retention schedule. The last thing you want is to be accused of is selective destruction. Many a company has found an unwelcome spot in the news headlines when they failed to destroy their records in a routine and consistent manner.

Destroying expired records on a monthly basis is a sound practice. Both the RIM manager and the records administrators should review their records each month, identifying records that are due for destruction. While RIM managers generally document off-site storage destruction, and all destruction processes should be documented, it is not necessary to document the destruction of every individual record. When in court, judges generally just want to ensure that all records are consistently kept for their proper retention period, no more and no less.

When penning the destruction policy, provide detailed instructions on how expired records are to be destroyed. Although it may cost a bit more to mandate the shredding of expired records, the mitigation of risk can make that extra cost worthwhile. Coordinate the destruction of electronic records with members of your IT department, as they might already have those practices in place. The following is the most widely used paper record destruction routine:

1. On the first business day of each month, the program manager runs a report of any and all records eligible for destruction. The report is then sent to each RA owning eligible inventory. When the report is sent, a firm deadline is established for each RA to respond.
2. The RA reviews the list to confirm that none of the records detailed on the destruction report are under a legal hold and that all records have indeed reached the proper destruction date.
3. Once the RA determines that the records scheduled for destruction should be destroyed, the RA emails the approval,

noting any necessary changes, to the DH and asks for approval. The DH indicates their approval and advises the RIM manager.
4. The RIM manager confirms with the off-site storage vendor which records are to be immediately destroyed.
5. The off-site vendor proceeds with destruction, then sends confirmation to the RIM manager that all records have been destroyed, as instructed.

In the audit section of this book, we will discuss following up on the destruction process.

CHAPTER THIRTEEN
TRAINING THE STAFF

Once all of the components of the program are in place, the staff must be adequately trained. All employees, regardless of their function, must understand every aspect of the RIM policy. For most, a quick webcast or in-house class will do the trick. Everyone from the CEO to the mail courier must have a complete understanding of their personal RIM responsibilities at the end of the training sessions. Each employee must receive a copy of the policy and sign an attestation stating that they understand and agree to abide by the policy.

In addition to policy training, DHs and RAs must receive in-depth training on record handling procedures. Make their jobs as easy as possible by giving them every crumb of relevant information that you can think of. Define their individual roles regard records handling, including monitoring and destruction processes.

All training must be documented. Document the name of each employee, the date that they were trained and specifically what kind of training each employee participated in. The documentation can be simple but it must be accurate. For a sample tracking sheet, see Appendix G.

Present the training sessions shortly before implementation day. Don't hold it too far in advance of release day because you don't want to lose the essential momentum that good training can create.

The form that the training takes will vary according to the size of the company and the available resources. If you are creating a program for a small company, classroom training should suffice. If yours is a larger company with several locations, a webcast might be the best choice. You could travel to each location and conduct classroom training but using webcasts is an effective and affordable alternative. In some rare cases, *i.e.,* for slow learners, one-on-one training might be required.

Whatever training method you choose, you must actually speak to your trainees. Do not simply hand them a copy of the policy and schedule and then expect them to grasp and/or care about the program. If you treat RIM program training as an afterthought, employees will treat the program as an afterthought.

Regardless of the training channels you choose, the training agenda should include:

➢ A review of the record retention policy. Each trainee should have a copy of the policy in front of them while it is being discussed. Don't read the policy to your students or you will put them to sleep. Just explain the basics and direct them to read it in full on their own at a later time.
➢ A demonstration of how to utilize the schedule. The schedule generally generates the most questions. Explain the basics of how it works and invite questions both

during the class and at any time in the future.
- A definition of certain terms. Surprisingly, the most asked question is usually, "What exactly is a record?" You might also have to define some other terms used in the policy. For example, it might be necessary to explain the difference between an active record and an inactive record.
- An explanation of how to use the off-site storage service that has been contracted. Include the basics of how to prepare records for storage, how to use the on-line system and how to retrieve boxes. For this part of the training, it is best to bring in a representative from the vendor and let them lead the session. Most vendors are more than happy to provide this service free of additional cost.
- A discussion of what a legal hold entails and what records handlers should do when they receive notice of a legal hold.
- An explanation of how the destruction processes will be carried out and what their duties may be in that process;
- Instructions on what to do if they need changes or additions made to the schedule;
- An explanation as to what costs each department can expect to incur for the storage, retrieval and destruction of their records;

- ➢ Clarification as to how to determine who the primary custodian is for any record;
- ➢ Guidance on how to audit their own records; and
- ➢ An explanation of scheduled and random program audits.

Your training handouts should include:

1. A copy of your presentation
2. A copy of the policy
3. A schedule of costs
4. The on-line system and procedure handbook
5. The RIM manager's contact information

Last but not least, work with the Human Resources department to make certain that this information is added to your new employee orientation and the annual code of business conduct refresher training.

CHAPTER FOURTEEN
THE BIG ROLLOUT

Now that you have all of the pieces of the program laid out, it's time to roll it out. Before you do so, outline each and every step of the implementation plan. Several tasks need to be tackled for a successful program rollout.

Publicize the Program

You already have the attention of managers and RAs but now you need to bring the rest of the staff onboard with the program. Many employees ignore company-wide emails, so inundate them in every way possible. Utilize posters, flyers, mass emails and any other means that may be at your disposal. Ask the DHs to hold 15-minute staff meetings to give a brief overview of the program and explain why participation is mandatory. Stress that all employees, no matter whether they're managing contracts or delivering the mail, will be expected to understand and comply with the retention policy.

Training

Train your RAs and DHs about a month before you train the rest of the staff. It is helpful for them to understand all aspects of the program so that they can answer questions from their co-workers.

Host mass training sessions at all of the company locations. Document training and follow up with those who do not participate.

Records Clean-Up Day

Give the staff an opportunity to make a fresh start. After everyone has been trained, host a company-wide clean-up day. Set aside a day or half-day to give them the opportunity to get rid of any expired or forbidden records that they might have in their possession. This helps to ensure compliance from day one by creating a controlled environment where employees have not only been given permission to destroy records but have actually been given the directive to destroy them. Many will hesitate to do so without a direct order.

All employees should be asked to review any records in their custody and then determine the proper handling of those records. At the end of the clean-up day, all employees should sign a certificate of understanding and compliance, certifying that they understand the policy and are in full compliance with all of its directives. See Appendix I for a sample form.

DHs should be directed to:

- Review the company policy to ensure the department is in compliance;
- Communicate clean-up day expectations to staff;
- Coordinate group efforts and ensure full compliance from all employees; and
- Stress to their staff the importance of participation and compliance.

RAs should be directed to:

- Communicate clean-up day expectations to department staff;
- Distribute retention schedules to all employees within the department;
- Maintain constant presence in the department during clean-up day in order to answer questions;
- Conduct spot-checks on employees to ensure records are appropriately stored or disposed of; and
- Gather completed compliance certification forms from employees and forward them to the RIM program manager for archiving.

Employees should be directed to:

- Review all records in their workspace and file cabinets in their areas;
- Dispose of unnecessary, forbidden or expired documents; and
- Complete a compliance certification form and submit it to their RAs/Supervisors.

The employees will have questions. Create a FAQ page and instruct the RAs to distribute it to each employee just prior to the clean-up day, along the with the certificate of understanding and compliance that you will find in Appendix H.

CHAPTER FIFTEEN
INSPIRING AND ENSURING COMPLIANCE

Another essential aspect of RIM program management is company-wide compliance with the established policies and procedures. It is also one of the most difficult aspects to manage. The corporate RIM program is often viewed as a troublesome and confusing issue that employees don't have the time, experience or incentive to deal with.

Financial sponsorship of the program can be a major concern. In today's economy, many corporations are decreasing expenditures rather than increasing them and most executives view a RIM initiative as an expensive undertaking with rather dubious value. Managers are often concerned about allocating their valuable staff hours to record management when their department already suffers from having too few employees to accomplish the tasks at hand.

When communicating with the executive team, highlight all aspects of compliance, including timely review and destruction. Many top executives mistakenly think that retaining everything forever will help avert the problems that some now infamous companies faced because problems were born as the result of improper destruction. However, the consequences of excessive retention must also be addressed.

Both executive and middle management employees relate well to a demonstration of potential cost savings. For example, if a program manager can demonstrate how investing eight hours of staff time in reviewing and purging files will save the department an impressive amount of money in the coming year, the DH will be much more willing to participate than if he is simply told that compliance is mandatory.

A picture is worth a thousand words and a black and white report of off-site storage costs provides managers with a very clear picture of their storage costs. When presented with this information, DHs are oftentimes shocked to learn that they were paying for off-site storage of records that they didn't realize existed.

Once the program has been rolled out, responsibility for the management of records, including the costs, should be allocated to individual departments and the RAs. Most people will heed the policies and monitor their storage costs much more efficiently when they know it comes out of their department budget. When it comes out of their budget, most managers will likewise start paying attention. Work with DHs to review their storage costs for previous years and help them prepare a strategy to reduce the costs allocated to their department. Once they see the RIM program as a way to trim their budget in a fairly painless way, they will be much more invested in the success of the program.

CHAPTER SIXTEEN
THE FUTURE:
DAY-TO-DAY MANAGEMENT

The honeymoon is over. The policy has been published, as has the retention schedule. The staff has been trained. The program has been implemented and everyone is on-board. Now what?

It is time to devise a plan for the continuing growth and success of the program. One part of the management plan was automatically created when you created the policy and defined the processes. Now is the time to thoroughly plan and execute a long-term vision for the program.

This is not the time to rest on your laurels. If the program is to succeed, you must continue to be vigilant. You must keep the communication channels between you and the RAs and DHs, as well as management, open and flowing. You are the program's greatest champion.

A great deal of your day will be spent performing liaison duties. When a records handler can't figure out how long to keep a record, you will be their all-knowing guide to the schedule. When an RA can't find a box of records that has been sent off-site, you will be the white knight who rushes in to track it down. You will be the center of the company's recordkeeping universe.

Those are your reactive duties. Your proactive duties include, but are not limited to, overseeing the destruction process, performing regular inventory audits and making sure that the schedule remains effective as regulations and your business change and grow.

Every month, you should send reminders to RAs to have on-site expired records destroyed. You will also coordinate and confirm off-site destruction with the vendor.

In order to justify your professional existence, as well as the budget, management will require activity and statistical reports. They will want you to track costs incurred, inventory movement, etc. Therefore, a huge portion of your day-to-day activities will include conducting record audits to confirm that everyone is complying with the program dictates as they should.

If you use an off-site vendor with a comprehensive web-based program, regular audits of what you have in storage should be a relatively simple matter of running reports from that website. When you run those reports, compare them to your latest destruction reports to confirm that the records that you ordered destroyed were in fact destroyed at the time and in the manner requested. You should also compare your reports against the monthly statement you receive from the off-site vendor.

On-site records will be a little more difficult and, at times, a little touchy. You will visit each department at least once a year and examine the records they have in their possession to ensure that they are not keeping expired or forbidden records. How those audits are structured will vary according to your business.

During the audits, look for expired documents, properly assigned destruction dates, properly assigned codes, forbidden records, etc. Violations should be reported to the department manager and resolution should be made within 30 days. Audits should begin approximately six months after the implementation of the program. You will conduct them alongside the DHs and the RAs. You don't need to check every record in the department but do conduct a random search of file cabinets, computer files, laptops, briefcases, etc.

Include new departments as they are created. Coach them on the policy and the procedures before they set up shop.

At the completion of each audit, both you and the department manager should sign off on the audit report. A simple memo stating that you either found no violations or that certain violations were found and properly addressed will suffice. If you do find violations, see to it that the DH addresses and corrects those problems within 30 days of notification. Use the form in Appendix K to track your auditing activities.

APPENDICES

APPENDIX A
THE MASTER PLAN

STEP	TASK	CHAPTER REFERENCE	DEADLINE
1	Obtain top tier Support	Four	
2	Establish executive committee	Five	
3	Develop basic policy	Seven	
4	Conduct records Inventory	Eight	
5	Create retention Schedule	Nine	
6	Select off-site storage vendor	Ten	
7	Develop legal hold System	Eleven	
8	Define document destruction Procedures	Twelve	
9	Train the staff	Thirteen	
10	Rollout program	Fourteen	
11	Build on your Momentum	Fifteen	On-going
12	Day-to-day Management	Sixteen	On-going

APPENDIX B
THE EXECUTIVE TEAM

DEPARTMENT	NAME	PHONE #

APPENDIX C
DEPARTMENT HEADS AND
RECORDS ADMINISTRATORS

DEPARTMENT	NAME	PHONE #

APPENDIX D
RECORD INVENTORY FORM

Name of document: _____

Created by: _____

Submitted to: _____

Processed by: _____

Storage location: _____

Active retention period: _____

Archive retention period: _____

Governing rule, if known: _____

Contractual obligation, if any: _____

Process Diagram

APPENDIX E
SAMPLE SCHEDULE

This is just a sample of what your retention schedule could resemble. Your completed schedule could include numerous record types. Depending on the size of the company and the number of record types you must maintain, you might also want to develop codes for each record type.

RECORD TYPE	DESCRIPTION	RETENTION PERIOD	FORMAT	RATIONALE
Brief description of the record type such as HR records, contracts, etc.	Full description of all records that fit the record type name	The long-term retention period as determined by your executive committee	Whether the records should be retained in paper or electronic format	Record of the contractual obligation or other rationale used to determine the proper retention period for these records

APPENDIX F
OFF-SITE VENDOR QUESTIONNAIRE

1. Does the vendor offer pick-up and delivery of the records? If so:
    a. What is the cost for a regularly scheduled pick-up or delivery?
    b. What is the cost for a rush delivery?
    c. What is the cost for a return?

2. Regarding the delivery trucks:
    a. What kind of security do they have on their trucks?
    b. Are the trucks marked with the vendor's name?
    c. Are the trucks secured each time the drivers leave the vehicles?

3. Visit the facility to see what type of security they offer.
    a. Do they have locked gates?
    b. Are the facilities fireproof and waterproof?
    c. Is staff on-site 24/7?
    d. Do they have security cameras covering every square inch of the facility?

4. Who handles the storage boxes? What are the hiring requirements for their staff?

5. What is the cost per cubic foot of storage?

6. Do they store out-of-the-ordinary shaped items? How?

7. Who pays for paper storage boxes or electronic media cases?

8. How are the boxes processed at the pick-up point?

9. How are boxes process upon arrival at the facility?

10. Will the company have a section of the facility devoted to your records or will they be mingled with those from other companies?

11. Does the vendor offer free on-line ordering of supplies and records?

12. Do you pay for boxes and labels or does the vendor provide them?

13. Can you contract for month-to-month service or must you sign a long-term contract? What happens if you must terminate a long-term contract before the term expires?

14. What other special services do they offer that could make your program more efficient?

15. Do they offer large volume discounts?

16. How do they track lost boxes? What problem resolution services does the vendor offer?

APPENDIX G
TRAINING RECORDS

SUBJECT	LOCATION	PARTICIPANT NAME	DATE COMPLETED

APPENDIX H
COMPLIANCE CERTIFICATION FORM

NOTE TO EMPLOYEES: PLEASE COMPLETE AND RETURN THIS FORM TO YOUR DEPARTMENT'S RECORD RETENTION ADMINISTRATOR BY THE CLOSE OF BUSINESS ON _____, ____.

I, _____, certify that I have participated in the _____, 20__ records clean-up day and that I am in full compliance with the (insert the company name) record retention policy.

_____   _____

Employee Signature   Date

APPENDIX I
AUDIT TRACKING

DEPARTMENT	AUDIT DATE	VIOLATIONS FOUND	COMPLIANCE CERTIFICATION DATE

Printed in Great Britain
by Amazon